Czech
COOKERY

slovart

OPEN SANDWICHES WITH HAM

- 1 baguette
  (or equivalent loaf
  of white bread)
- butter
- 200 g potato salad
  made with mayonnaise
- 150 g thinly sliced ham
  (circles)
- 1 tin of sardines
- 2–3 peeled hard-boiled
  eggs
- 150 g processed cheese
- a few pickled
  cucumbers
- ½ a pickled red pepper
- parsley

❶ Remove the ends of the loaf and cut it into 1 cm thick slices. Spread each thinly with butter, sprinkle with salt according to taste and add a layer of potato salad.
❷ Make a cut from the edge to the centre in each slice of ham, and twist into a cone shape. Drain the sardines. Cut the eggs into slices.
❸ Place a ham cone on each slice of bread and potato salad, adding a piece of sardine, slice of egg and piece of cheese. Decorate with a little fan of pickled cucumber, a ribbon of red pepper and a sprig of parsley.

Note: You can also decorate the open ham sandwiches with pieces of vegetables, such as fresh green, yellow or red pepper, slices of tomato, olives and thin slices of hard cheese. For home-made potato salad see the recipe on p. 24.

PRAGUE HAM WITH CREAMED HORSERADISH

- 100 g fresh cream
  cheese
- 4 tablespoons finely
  grated horseradish
- 125 ml whipping
  cream
- pinch of salt
- 4 slices of ham
- 1 tomato
- parsley

❶ Mash the cheese and mix with the grated horseradish and salt.
❷ Whip the chilled cream and stir lightly into the cheese and horseradish.
❸ Put the slices of ham on a board, place dollops of creamed horseradish in the centre of each and roll them up. Arrange the rolls on a plate, decorate with slices of tomato and sprigs of parsley.

Note: You can arrange the rolls on fresh green lettuce leaves.

Open Sandwiches with Ham (above) and Prague Ham with Creamed Horseradish

3

HOME-MADE COLLARED PORK

- *1 pork knee chopped in half*
- *1 pork tongue*
- *salt*
- *150 g pig's liver*
- *200 g pork meat (any cut)*
- *1 teaspoon whole pepper corns*
- *1 teaspoon old spice*
- *ground pepper*

❶ Place the pork knee and tongue in a saucepan, cover with cold water, add salt and boil until soft. Strain off the liquid and reserve. Rinse the tongue and peel off the skin. Remove the bones from the knee, then place the skin from the knee, the pork meat and the whole spices in the reserved liquid and boil until almost soft. Add the liver and boil until soft. Strain off the liquid and reserve.

❷ Test the liquid (pour a little onto a plate and let it set into jelly). If too runny, boil the rest of the liquid hard until part of it has evaporated. If too thick, thin out the liquid by adding a little hot water and boiling for a short time.

❸ Cut the skin, the meat from the knee, the pork meat, tongue and liver into small pieces. Mix into the liquid, add salt and pepper. Wrap the mixture in muslin or foil, securing the "bag" at both ends with string.

❹ Boil water in a saucepan. Attach the string at both ends of the "bag" to a wooden spoon, and then place the spoon across the top of a saucepan, allowing the collared pork to hang in the boiling water without touching the bottom of the saucepan. Simmer for 40 minutes, and then turn the collared pork over and simmer for another 30 minutes.

❺ Place the collared pork on a board, press it down (e. g. by placing another board and weight on top of it), and leave to set overnight. Serve slices of the collared pork with onion and watered vinegar. And of course beer.

VARIATION

You can make brawn in the same way. You need 4 pig's trotters, 400 g pork meat (any cut), salt, a few whole black peppers and all strained spice, 3 bay leaves, a pinch of thyme, 1 onion, 2 carrots, a piece of celeriac and a piece of parsnip. Boil the trotters in salted water until soft. Drain off the liquid, reserve and leave to cool, then skim off the fat. Place the skin from the trotters, the pork meat and the spices in a saucepan, pour the liquid over them, add the vegetables and boil until soft. Cut the skin and meat into pieces, add sliced carrot, and the liquid. Place in baking forms or bowls and leave to set in a cool place.

Home-made Collared Pork and Brawn (on the right)

BOILED SMOKED PORK WITH APPLE HORSERADISH AND BEETROOT

- *600 g smoked pork fore loin*

For the apple horseradish
- *1 large apple*
- *castor sugar*
- *salt*
- *vinegar or lemon juice*

- *4 cm piece horseradish*

For the beetroot
- *3 small beetroots*
- *3 cm piece horseradish*
- *castor sugar*
- *salt*
- *wine vinegar*

❶ Put the smoked pork in a saucepan of hot water and bring to the boil. Simmer for 3 minutes and then drain off the water. Pour more hot water onto the pork and boil it until soft.

❷ Drain off the liquid, bone the meat and slice it thinly against the grain.

❸ For the apple horseradish, peel, core and grate the apple, and immediately mix it with the sugar, salt and vinegar or lemon juice. Scrub the horseradish, grate it finely into the apple, mix lightly and season more if desired.

❹ Boil the beetroot until soft, drain it, rinse it immediately in cold water and peel. Finely grate the beetroot and flavour with sugar, salt and vinegar.

❺ Serve the boiled smoked pork hot with the apple horseradish, beetroot, various kinds of mustard and (if you like) cold spicy sauces.

Note: You can also serve boiled smoked pork with mashed potatoes or peas, lentils or beans, or spinach and boiled potatoes. When cold, thin slices of the smoked pork make an excellent addition to a plate of cold cuts, or in sandwiches.

VARIATION
Instead of cooked smoked pork fore loin you can use pork knee. Boil it with salt, several peppercorns, allspice, juniper berries and a bay leaf. Leftover boiled smoked pork can also be used effectively in a baked pasta dish. All you have to do is cut it into small pieces and mix it with already cooked squares of pasta (or other pasta shapes) and beaten eggs, sprinkle with chopped chives and bake it in the oven until golden. The same recipe could be used replacing pasta with boiled sliced potatoes.

BEEF SOUP WITH HOME-MADE NOODLES

- 400 g stewing beef
- 1–2 slender beef bones
- salt
- a few peppercorns and whole allspice
- 1 bay leaf
- 1 small onion
- 200 g root vegetables (carrots, celeriac, parsnip)
- parsley

For the home-made noodles
- 100 g medium fine flour
- 1 egg
- 1 teaspoon of oil
- 1 tablespoon of warm water
- flour for rolling

❶ Place the meat and bones in a pressure cooker and cover with cold water, season with salt, add spices and bring to the boil. Place the lid on tight and simmer for 30 minutes. Then open the pressure cooker and if the meat is almost soft, add the onion and sliced vegetables. Close the pressure cooker again and boil for a further 5 minutes.

❷ **For the home-made noodles:** Sieve the flour. Beat the eggs with the oil, water and two teaspoons of flour. Put the rest of the flour in a heap on a board and make a hollow in the mound. Pour the egg mixture into the hollow and then mix it with the flour using an ordinary table knife (i.e. without a sharp tip), to produce a dough which you finish off by kneading with your hands. Divide the dough into two parts and roll each into a thin sheet. Allow to dry off, and then turn over, allowing the reverse side to dry off. Then cut the dough into ribbons 4 cm. wide, fold and cut into thin noodles. Leave on the board to dry out, and then boil and drain.

❸ Strain the soup and then add sliced carrot, noodles, and some of the meat pieces. Decorate with chopped parsley.

VARIATION

Liver Dumplings: Remove the membrane from either beef, pig or chicken liver (approx. 100 g) and mince finely. Add 2 tablespoons of melted butter, an egg, garlic mashed with salt, a pinch of marjoram and pepper, 2 tablespoons of coarse ground flour. Mix and if necessary add bread-crumbs to thicken. Take spoonfuls of the mixture and simmer them in the soup. **Marrow dumplings:** To the melted and sieved marrow (approx. 2 tablespoons) add an egg, salt, mace and 1 tbsp of coarse ground flour. Mix and if necessary add bread-crumbs to thicken. Take spoonfuls of the mixture and simmer them in the soup.

Beef Soup with Home-made Noodles (below), and Soup with Liver Dumplings

9

GARLIC SOUP (OUKROP)

- *8–12 cloves of garlic*
- *salt*
- *2 slices of black bread*
- *2 tablespoons of goose fat or oil*
- *700 ml meat stock*
- *parsley*

❶ Crush the garlic with salt. Cut the bread into strips or cubes and fry them in oil. Distribute the bread and garlic mixture in individual plates.

❷ Heat up the stock, pour it into the plates, and scatter finely chopped parsley on top. **Note:** To make the soup more substantial you could add boiled sliced potato, or slices of smoked sausage or diced salami. Another variation is to stir 1–2 eggs into the soup.

TRIPE SOUP

- *1 medium onion*
- *3 tablespoons oil*
- *80 g medium fine flour*
- *800 ml water*
- *1 bouillon cube*
- *1 tablespoon oil*
- *2 tablespoons paprika*
- *500 g cooked tripe, cut in pieces*
- *3–4 cloves of garlic*
- *salt*
- *marjoram*
- *hot pepper (ground)*

❶ Melt the oil in a saucepan, add the finally chopped onion and flour and make a roux. Thin it with hot water and stir well on a low heat until smooth. Add a crumbled bouillon cube and boil for 10 minutes.

❷ Heat more oil and add paprika, then pour this into the soup, add the tripe and bring to the boil. Season the soup with garlic mashed with salt, marjoram and hot pepper to taste. Serve with bread rolls or slices of black bread.
Note: You can also use coarsely grated carrot, celeriac or parsnip in this soup, or strips of green pepper; add these ingredients to the roue at the beginning. Sprinkle the soup with chopped chives before serving.

Garlic Soup (above) and Tripe Soup

POTATO SOUP

- *300 g peeled potatoes*
- *200 g vegetables (carrots, celeriac, leeks, curly cabbage)*
- *10 g dried mushrooms*
- *1 small onion*
- *3 tablespoons oil*
- *40 g medium fine flour*
- *700 ml water*
- *salt*
- *2–3 cloves of garlic*
- *marjoram*
- *chives*

❶ Cut the potatoes and vegetables into small pieces. Soak the dried mushrooms in warm water.
❷ Heat the oil in a saucepan and add the onion and flour to create a white roux, add the water, gradually increase the heat and stir until smooth. Add the potatoes, vegetables and mushrooms, season with salt and simmer until soft.
❸ Add the finelly chopped garlic and marjoram and simmer a little longer. Decorate with chopped chives.
Note: This soup can be modified according to the season e. g. by adding scalded, peeled and chopped tomato or fresh boletus mushrooms.

MUSHROOM SOUP (KULAJDA)

- *250 g fresh mushrooms*
- *2 tablespoons of oil*
- *salt*
- *1/2 teaspoon of caraway seeds*
- *700 ml water*
- *1 tablespoon oil*
- *50 g medium fine flour*
- *castor sugar*
- *wine vinegar*
- *2 tablespoons of finely chopped dill*
- *200 ml sour cream*

❶ Finely slice the mushrooms, sauté them in oil, add water, salt and caraway and stew until soft.
❷ Heat the oil, add flour and mix, and then gradually add hot water and stir until smooth. Boil for 15 minutes.
❸ Add the mushrooms, bring back to the boil, add sugar and vinegar to taste, stir in the dill and simmer for a short time.
❹ Stir the cream into the soup and heat through, but do not boil.
Note: Halved hard-boiled eggs can be placed in the serving-plates. Pour the soup over them and decorate with chopped chives.

Potato Soup (above) and Mushroom Soup

BOILED BEEF WITH TOMATO SAUCE AND BREAD DUMPLINGS

- boiled beef (see recipe on p. 8)

For the tomato sauce
- 1 small onion
- 2 tablespoons of oil
- 50 g medium fine flour
- 500 ml beef stock (fresh or using stock cube)
- several peppercorns and allspice
- 2 bay leaves
- pinch of thyme
- a piece of cinnamon
- 2 tablespoons of castor sugar
- 1 tin tomato puree (80 g)
- salt
- wine vinegar

For the bread dumplings
- 400 g coarse flour
- 15 g yeast
- approx. 150 ml milk
- 1 egg yolk
- salt
- flour for rolling
- 2 white bread rolls, slightly stale

❶ The tomato sauce:
Heat the oil and add chopped onion and flour to create a roux. Thin with stock and stir until smooth. Add spices and simmer for 15 minutes.
❷ Moisten the sugar with water and heat in a pan until caramelised. Thin with a little water and reheat.
❸ Strain the sauce, mix with tomato puree, caramel, salt, and vinegar, and simmer briefly.

❹ The bread dumplings:
Sieve the flour into a bowl, crumble the yeast into it, add 2 tablespoons warm milk and mix into a dough, adding more flour if necessary. Cover the bowl. When the dough has risen, add the egg-yolk and salt, and work it into a thicker dough with the remaining milk. Dust with flour, cover and leave to rise.
❺ Dice the rolls and work them into the risen dough. Divide the dough into two parts and roll each into a long cylindrical dumpling. Place in boiling salted water and boil for 25 minutes. Take the dumplings out the water and cut them into slices using a thread.
❻ Serve the sauce with the boiled meat and bread dumplings.

VARIATION
Dill sauce can be used instead of tomato sauce. Mix 4 tablespoons of flour with 300 ml of cold stock and bring to the boil while stirring continuously. Add salt and sugar and simmer for 15 minutes. Stir in 4 tablespoons of chopped dill, simmer for a short time, add lemon juice to taste and 200 ml of sour cream.

FILLET STEAK WITH CREAM SAUCE AND BREAD DUMPLINGS

- *700 g fillet steak or beef shoulder (with fat removed)*
- *100 g bacon*
- *1 medium onion*
- *salt*
- *250 g chopped root vegetables (carrot, celeriac, parsnip)*
- *1 teasp. peppercorns*
- *several whole allspice and juniper berries*
- *pinch of thyme*
- *2 bay leaves*
- *2 tblesp. castor sugar*
- *1 tblesp. medium flour*
- *lemon juice*
- *200 ml sour cream*
- *stewed cranberries or cranberry jam*
- *bread dumplings (recipe on p. 14)*

❶ Trim the meat and lard with strips of bacon. Sauté the remaining bacon with the onion, add the meat, brown it all over, season with salt, add hot water and stew until almost soft.

❷ Add vegetables and spices and stew until soft.

❸ Moisten the sugar and heat in a pan until caramelised. Dilute it by boiling with a little water.

❹ Take out the soft meat and cover to keep it warm. Put the vegetables and liquid through a sieve or blende (having removed the whole spices). Add the diluted caramel and flour mixed with a little cold water. Bring to the boil and simmer for a few minutes. Add lemon juice Take off the heat, beat in the sour cream and reheat (but donot boil or it will curdle).

❺ Cut the meat into slices, arrange on serving plates and decorate with rounds of lemon and cranberries. Serve the sauce separately. Bread dumplings are the best accompaniment to Fillet with Cream Sauce.

Lard the meat using a sharp-tipped knife to insert strips of bacon.

Pass the vegetables and liquid through a sieve, or remove the spices and blend.

ROAST PORK WITH STEWED SAURKRAUT AND POTATO DUMPLINGS

Number of Portions: 4–6 ✳ ✳ ✳

- 600 g pork neck or shoulder
- salt
- caraway

For the stewed sauerkraut
- 30 g lard
- 1 medium onion
- 500 g sauerkraut in its liquid
- caraway
- salt

- castor sugar

For the bread dumplings
- 800 g boiled peeled potatoes
- 1 teaspoon salt
- 50 g cornflour
- 1 egg
- 50 g semolina
- approx. 100 g coarse ground flour

❶ Place the meat in a baking pan, sprinkle with salt and caraway. Add half a glass of water, cover, place in the oven and roast, occasionally basting the meat with its own juices and adding hot water. After 40 minutes take off the cover, turn the meat over and roast until soft.

❷ **Stewed Sauerkraut:** Sauté the sliced onion in the lard, add the sauerkraut and its liquid and the caraway, and stew uncovered. Add a little hot water as necessary during stewing.

❸ Add salt and sugar to the soft sauerkraut to taste, and complete stewing.

❹ Grate the potatoes onto a board, add salt, sprinkle with cornflour,

make a hollow in the middle and add the egg. Work into a dough with a blunt ended knife while gradually adding semolina and flour.

❺ Divide the dough into four parts of equal size. Roll them into thick sausage shapes, place them in boiling water and simmer for 15–20 minutes. Take them out using a perforated ladle and cut them in slices.

Note: While stewing the sauerkraut you can add a medium-sized peeled and finely grated potato (this is Moravian method).

VARIATION

Instead of potato dumplings, you can serve "hairy" dumplings made of raw potato. To make these take 800 g of peeled and finely grated potatoes, mix them with salt, a tablespoon of cornflour and 250 g of coarse-ground flour. Take spoonfuls of the mixture using a table spoon dipped in water, and place them in boiling salted water. Simmer for 8–10 minutes depending on size.

Work the potato dough using a knife with a curved end.

Divide the flour into four equal parts and make them into rolls.

19

ROAST GOOSE WITH STEWED WHITE CABBAGE AND DUMPLINGS

- *young goose*
- *salt*
- *caraway*

For the stewed white cabbage
- *600 g white cabbage*
- *salt*

- *caraway*
- *castor sugar*
- *wine vinegar*
- *bread dumplings*
  (for recipe see p. 14)
- *or potato dumplings*
  (for recipe see p. 18)

❶ Rub the goose's cavity with salt, place it in a roasting dish breast down, sprinkle with salt and caraway, add a little water, cover and roast for approx. ¾ of an hour. Then roast uncovered, occasionally basting with its own juices and adding hot water. If the goose is particularly fat, pierce the skin in the fattier parts and skim the fat off.

❷ When almost soft, turn the goose over and then complete roasting.

❸ **Stewed white cabbage:** Shred the cabbage, season with salt and caraway, and add water. Stew until soft. When soft add sugar and salt according to taste.

❹ Put the goose on a cutting board, cut it into portions using scissors, and arrange on a heated serving plate. Serve the roasting juices, stewed white cabbage and one or both types of dumpling separately. **Note:** You can serve stewed red cabbage instead, or both kinds of cabbage at once. Shred the red cabbage, add salt and caraway, pour on a little red wine and stew until almost soft. Then add some grated apple, flavour to taste with sugar and vinegar, add more wine and stew until soft. Goose liver is a particular delicacy. Remove all the membranes, add several peeled almonds and roast until soft in goose fat. Then season with salt, add more fat as needed and allow to set.

VARIATION

Duck may be roasted in the same way as goose. First you should stuff it using a mixture of ground pork and beef mixed with finely diced white bread moistened with wine. Season the stuffing with salt and add ground caraway and finely chopped parsley. The duck should be cut into 4–6 portions. You could also stuff the goose or duck with apples before roasting, since this gives a special extra aroma.

HOME PIG-FEAST

For the sausage meat
- ½ pig's head
- 1 pig's knee and tongue
- salt
- 2 white bread rolls
- 250 g pig's liver
- 1 teaspoon whole peppercorns and whole allspice
- marjoram
- garlic
- liver sausage
- black pudding
- lard

For the sauerkraut salad
- 600 g sauerkraut
- 1 tablespoon castor sugar
- salt
- 2 tablespoons oil
- 1 medium red apple

❶ **Sausage meat:** Put the pig's head, knee and tongue in a pan, cover with cold water, add salt and boil until soft. Drain (reserving the stock), rinse the tongue in cold water and skin it.

❷ When cooled, bone the meat and skim the fat from the stock. Soak the crumbled bread in some of the stock.

❸ Coarsely grind the meat, tongue and liver (after removing membranes), with the soaked bread. Add the fat skimmed off the stock, salt, fresh-ground pepper and allspice, marjoram and crushed garlic. Thin the mixture with a little stock as necessary, mix well. Spread the mixture in a thick layer in an ovenproof pan and roast.

❹ **Sauerkraut salad:** Drain and chop the sauerkraut. Dissolve the sugar in the sauerkraut liquid, add salt, and mix the liquid with the oil into the sauerkraut. Core the apple, cube, and mix with the sauerkraut.

❺ Arrange the sausage meat, liver sausage and black pudding on a serving plate. Serve with boiled potatoes or just with fresh bread and sauerkraut salad.

Note: You could also mix 2–3 tablespoons of finely grated horseradish into the salad. If you warm the liver sausage and blood sausage in hot water before roasting them in fat, you reduce the risk of the skin bursting.

VARIATION

You can diversify the pig-feast plate by also serving roast bratwurst (also warmed in hot water before roasting) and thin cutlets. The sausage meat tastes just as good cold. Serve it cut into slices with finely grated horseradish, and sterilised beetroot, cucumber pickles or onions, different kinds of mustard and either cabbage or potato salad (see recipe on p. 24), as well as black bread.

FRIED CARP
WITH POTATO SALAD

- *8 portions of carp*
- *salt*
- *fine ground flour*
- *2 eggs*
- *bread-crumbs*
- *oil for frying*
- *4 slices of lemon*
- *parsley*

For the potato salad
- *600 g boiled peeled potatoes*
- *salt*
- *pepper*
- *300 ml mixed pickled vegetables*
- *150 g mayonnaise*

❶ Sprinkle the carp portions with salt, cover and leave in a cool place for half an hour. Then roll them in a mixture of flour, beaten egg and bread-crumbs, and fry them in oil until golden. Arrange them on a serving plate and decorate with slices of lemon and a sprig of parsley.

❷ **Potato salad:** Dice the potatoes and season with salt and pepper. Drain the pickled vegetables, add them to the potatoes and stir with some of the vegetable liquid. Then stir in the mayonnaise. Leave the salad to chill in a cool place.

Note: The potato salad will be less rich if you replace part of the mayonnaise with sour cream or plain yoghurt, in both cases adding 1–2 spoonfuls of quality oil. You can replace the pickled mixed vegetables with diced carrot and peas boiled in salted water, and add finely chopped pickled cucumber and fresh grated onion. Another variation of the potato salad can be made with peas and beans boiled in salted water and cubed peeled apples and onions. You can also add ham cut into small pieces. If you prefer a simpler and less fatty version of the carp recipe, just sprinkle salt on the portions, dust with fine flour and bake slowly in butter.

VARIATION
For children or those who dislike fish, fried carp – which is the traditional Czech Christmas food – can be replaced by fried chicken breasts. Cut the meat into slices, beat them slightly flatter and sprinkle with salt and pepper. Beat the egg with a little white wine. Roll the meat in flour, egg and, bread-crumbs, and fry until golden in the oil. Dry the meat on a paper towel, dot with melted butter and decorate with slices of lemon.

RABBIT ROLL
WITH BOILED POTATOES

Number of Portions: 6–8   ✳ ✳ ✳

- saddle of rabbit with breast and haunches
- rabbit liver
- 60 g butter
- 1/2 white bread roll
- 100 g belly pork
- 1 egg
- salt
- pinch of grated nutmeg
- 2 tablespoons of chopped parsley
- 1 large onion
- 1/2 teaspoon of pepper corns
- several whole allspice
- 200 ml white wine
- 400 g vegetables (carrots, celeriac, leek)

For the boiled potatoes
- 1,2 kg peeled potatoes
- salt
- several leaves of lovage
- 40 g butter
- parsley

❶ Remove membrane from saddle and breast, bone and trim to make a flat rectangle. Remove membrane from haunches and bone. Cut one haunch into thin strips.

❷ Remove membrane from liver, slice and roast in half the butter. Crumble the bread and moisten with a little wine.

❸ Chop up the belly pork and meat from the second haunch, mince, and then mince again with the bread. Mix with the egg, salt, nutmeg and chopped parsley.

Spread the mixture on the rectangle of meat and place the strips of haunch and liver on top. Roll up the rectangle and secure with strong thread.

❹ Soften the chopped onion in the remaining butter in a roasting pan, place the roll on top,

season with salt, add bones and spices, pour in the wine and roast in the oven until almost soft, occasionally basting the meat with its own juices and more wine.

❺ Take out the roll and strain the juices back into the pan. Add the chopped vegetables and a little salt, put the roll back and complete roasting.

❻ Cut up the potatoes, place in hot water, add salt and lovage and boil until soft. Drain, dot with butter and toss with parsley.

❼ Remove the roll from the oven and cut into slices. Serve garnished with the vegetables and potatoes.

VARIATION
Boned chicken can be used instead of rabbit. Make the stuffing using belly pork, any cut of pork, and chicken livers. Trim the chicken meat into a rectangle with the skin still attached, and stuff in the same way as for the rabbit roll.

Spread the rectangle of meat with stuffing and add strips of meat and liver.

Roll up the meat and secure with strong thread to ensure the roll keeps its shape.

27

BEEF GOULASH
WITH BREAD DUMPLINGS

Number of Portions: 4–6   ✳ ✳

- 600 g stewing beef
- 100 g bacon
- 4 large onions
- 2 tablespoons paprika
- salt
- ½ teaspoon caraway
- marjoram

- 2 tablespoons medium fine flour
- garlic
- hot pepper
- bread dumplings (for recipe see p. 14)

❶ Cut the meat into chunks. Sauté the chopped onion and bacon in a pan. Add the meat, brown it and sprinkle with paprika. Stir and pour on a little hot water, add salt and stew until almost soft. Boil off the liquid until only fat remains, sprinkle with flour, brown, add water and stew until soft.

❷ Season the meat with marjoram, mashed garlic and hot paprika to taste, and then stew for a short time.

❸ Serve the beef goulash with bread dumplings. Decorate with a sprig of parsley, a spoonful of sour cream or thin rounds of onion.

Note: Do not roast the paprika, because it would become dark and bitter. Goulash can also be made from equal quantities of meat and onions sliced into rounds. Instead of flour, dry bread crumbs can be used to thicken the goulash. The dish can also be served with boiled rice or pasta, or we can surprise our guests by serving it in a hollowed out loaf of bread. Just slice off the top of the loaf, hollow out the bread, fill with goulash and put the top back on. Large crusty rolls can also by used for individual portions. Serve with a side salad as a warming winter dish.

VARIATION

In the last stages of stewing the goulash you could also add strips of red pepper, 2–3 scalded peeled and chopped onions and peeled diced potato, producing a thick goulash soup to be served with fresh bread. Finely sliced and sautéd fresh mushrooms, best of all boletus, will give your goulash a different flavour. Another variant is to add pre-cooked large or small white beans to the goulash, with a finely chopped chilli pepper and a little ketchup.

Beef Goulash with Bread Rolls (above) and Goulash Soup

BEEF ROLLS
WITH MASHED POTATO

Number of Portions: 4 ✱✱

- 4 flat pieces of stewing steak
- salt
- pepper
- mustard
- 4 rounds of ham salami or ham
- 1 small onion
- 1 hard-boiled peeled egg
- 1–2 pickled cucumbers

- 80 g bacon
- 30 g butter
- 1 tablespoon medium flour

For the mashed potato
- 800 g peeled potatoes
- salt
- approx. 200 ml milk
- 30 g butter
- parsley

❶ Beat the meat to flatten slightly, season with salt and pepper, spread with mustard, and arrange the salami or ham, pieces of onion, quarters of eggs and pickled cucumber slices on top. Roll up and secure with needles.

❷ Melt the finely chopped bacon over the heat, add the rolls and brown, add salt and water and stew until soft. Lift out the rolls and remove the needles.

❸ Make a liaison with the butter and flour, add to the stewing juices in pieces and allow to dissolve. Replace the rolls and heat through.

❹ **Mashed potatoes:** Cut up the potatoes, cover with hot water, season with salt and boil until soft. Then drain and mash, gradually adding warm milk, butter and more salt to taste. Mash to a smooth consistency.

❺ Serve the rolls with the mashed potato sprinkled with parsley.
Note: Cream may be added to the mashed potato instead of milk.

Arrange salami or ham, onion, egg quarters and cucumber on the meat.

An electric beater makes it easier to mash the potatoes with the milk and butter.

PHEASANT WITH BACON ON MUSHROOM RICE

- *1 pheasant*
- *salt*
- *100 g bacon*
- *1 small onion*
- *a few peppercorns, grains of allspice and juniper berries*
- *1–2 bay leaves*
- *30 g butter*

For the mushroom rice
- *30 g butter*
- *150 g mushrooms*
- *300 g long-grain rice*
- *parsley*

❶ Rub the inside of the pheasant with salt. Fix two slices of bacon to the breast with needles to prevent the meat drying out during roasting.

❷ Finely chop the rest of the bacon, melt it in a roasting dish and sauté the onion. Add the pheasant and brown on both sides. Add hot water, salt and spices. Roast until soft, occasionally basting in its own juices.

❸ **Mushroom Rice:** Brown the sliced mushrooms in hot butter. Rinse the rice first with cold and then hot water. Drain it, add salt, mix with the mushroom, add water and stew until soft. Shake the pan several times during the cooking.

❹ Chop the parsley finely and add to the rice.

❺ Sieve the roasting juices from the pheasant and heat them up with the butter.

❻ Cut the pheasant into portions and arrange on a plate, topping with the slices of roast bacon and surrounding with servings of rice. The pheasant can also be served with stewed pears and cranberries or rowan berries.

Note: The rice can be flavoured in several different ways. Add cooked peas and finely chopped parsley, or chopped ham or 1 tblesp. of curry powder, perhaps with raisins and chopped peeled almonds.

VARIATION

Stuff the pheasant before roasting with 2–3 small apples, and serve with halved apples. Or try almond stuffing: beat the eggs with a tablespoon of melted butter, add salt, a teaspoon of mixed spice, diced toasted bread, chopped parboiled carrot, 30 g of almond kernels and chopped parsley. Mix, stuff the pheasant and secure the opening with strong thread, to be removed before cutting the pheasant into portions, and arranging on a serving dish.

RUMP OF VENISON
WITH WINE AND POTATO CROQUETTES

- rump of venison
- salt
- 100 g bacon
- 1 medium onion
- 200 g root vegetables (carrot, celeriac, parsnip)
- several peppercorns, grains of allspice and juniper berries
- approx. 200 ml of red wine
- 1 tablespoon castor sugar
- 1 tablespoon medium flour
- lemon juice

For the potato croquettes
- 1,2 kg peeled boiled potatoes
- 2 tablespoons cornflour
- salt
- pinch of mace
- 2 tablespoons finely chopped parsley
- 60 g butter
- 3 egg yolks
- approx. 20 g coarse flour
- 2 egg whites
- bread-crumbs
- oil for frying

❶ Remove the membrane from the meat and season with salt. Cut some of the bacon into strips and lard the meat with it. Chop the rest of the bacon finely, melt in a pan, add the chopped onion and diced vegetables and brown them. Add the meat, with the pepper, allspice and juniper. Add some of the wine and roast, occasionally basting the meat with its own juices and adding more wine.

❷ Moisten the sugar with water and roast until golden and caramelised. Dissolve in two tablespoons of water.

❸ Take out the soft meat. Put the vegetables through a sieve, or remove the spices and blend. Stir the flour into the remaining wine, and add to the vegetable puree with the caramel.

Simmer the sauce for a little, season with salt and add lemon juice according to taste.

❹ **Potato croquettes:** Grate the potatoes, sprinkle them with the sieved cornflour, salt, mace and parsley. Make a hollow in the middle and add the softened butter and egg yolks, and knead to a smooth dough. Cut it into portions of equal size and roll them into cylinders. Dip these in the whipped egg, roll in bread-crumbs and fry in hot oil until golden.

❺ Cut the meat into slices and arrange on a serving dish. Serve the potato croquettes and sauce separately.

Note: One tasty variant is to add two tablespoons of red-currant jelly and cranberries to the sauce. Decorate the meat with lemon and rowan or cranberries.

POTATO PANCAKES (BRAMBORÁK)

- *800 g peeled potatoes*
- *salt*
- *several cloves of garlic*
- *ground caraway*
- *marjoram*
- *1 egg*
- *approx. 100 g medium flour*
- *lard or oil for frying*

❶ Grate the potatoes finely, season with salt and add crushed garlic, caraway and marjoram to taste. Add the egg and flour and combine into a thick mixture.

❷ Heat the lard or oil in a pan. Add part of the mixture and spread. Fry slowly on both sides. Repeat.

❸ Serve the pancakes hot, while they are still crispy, and with beer or tea.

Note: To prevent the grated potato discolouring, pour off part of the liquid produced by grating, add a little hot milk and mix. Always make your pancakes as thin as possible, so that they are crispy. If you replace part of the flour with bread-crumbs, they will be even crispier.

You can ring the changes on the potato dough, for example by replacing a quarter of the dough with finely grated carrot, marrow, celeriac or unpeeled apple. Or else by adding little pieces of salami or thin rounds of sausage, placed on the mixture and fried with it, and perhaps with a little finely ground crackling. Another variant is to add drained, chopped sauerkraut or fresh cabbage, with mushrooms stewed with cumin. Little potato pancakes made in a griddle pan can be served with boiled smoked meat (see recipe on p. 6), pork or lamb cutlets, or poultry with stewed sauerkraut (see recipe on p. 18). Potato pancake mixture spread thickly on a pan greased with lard and baked in the oven is called "shaky pie" or "smash".

VARIATION
Potato pancakes can be filled in various ways after frying: put stewed mushrooms or cooked meat leftovers on one half of the pancake, cover with the other half and sprinkle with grated cheese and finely chopped chives or parsley. Serve with beer.

POTATO FLATCAKES

- 800 g cold potatoes boiled in their skins and then peeled
- ½ teaspoon of salt
- approx. 150 g fine flour
- lard or butter for spreading

Sweet version
- damson-cheese
- grated cream cheese
- sour cream or plain yoghurt for decoration

❶ Finely grate the boiled potatoes onto a board, season with salt and gradually add the sieved flour. Work into a smooth doughy mixture. Cut into equal sized parts and roll them into flat rounds on a floured surface.

❷ Using a cast iron griddle on a gas burner, or a dry teflon pan, slowly cook the flat cakes on both sides. When cooked, spread them with a little melted lard or butter and stack them on a plate set above a pan of hot water, to keep them warm.

❸ Spread the flatcakes with damson-cheese, sprinkle with grated hard-cheese, and serve them decorated with a blob of sour cream or plain yoghurt.

Note: Potato flat cakes can also be served as a savoury. They taste wonderful with boiled smoked meat (see recipe on p. 6), roast pork (recipe on p. 18) roast goose (recipe on p. 20) or duck with stewed sauerkraut (recipe on p. 18), or just with hot smoked bacon or crackling. As a meatless dish they can be served with sauerkraut salad (recipe on p. 22), steamed spinach or mangold. Potato flatcakes can also be fried in hot oil.

Slice the dough into pieces of equal size and roll them out into rounds.

Slowly cook the rounds on both sides on a cast-iron griddle or pan.

Potato Flat Cakes both Sweet (above) and Savoury with Crackling

POTATO PASTA BALLS (ŠKUBÁNKY)

- *800 g peeled potatoes*
- *salt*
- *150–200 g medium flour*
- *powdered poppy-seed*
- *or grated gingerbread for sprinkling*
- *icing sugar*
- *butter or lard*

❶ Chop up the potatoes, and boil in salted water for approximately 15 minutes. Then drain, pouring the water back into the pan. Partially mash the potatoes and make several holes in the mixture with a reversed wooden spoon. Sprinkle with sieved flour and put them in a pan with a little less than $2/3$ of the water in which they were boiled. Cover the pan, turn down the heat to the minimum, and steam the potatoes for approx. 20 minutes.

❷ Work the potatoes with the flour thoroughly until you have a thick smooth paste. If it is too thick, thin with a little of the remaining potato water. Add salt according to taste.

❸ Make the balls by taking spoonfuls of the paste with a spoon dipped in melted butter or lard, put them on a plate and sprinkle with powdered poppy-seed or grated gingerbread. Add a little sugar and dot with melted butter or lard.

Note: Make sure you work the paste long enough to get rid of all the lumps of potato.

Spoon out any remaining mixture, cover, and put in the refridgerator. The next day you can fry the balls in hot oil until golden and serve them as a savoury snack with finely chopped golden-fried bacon and onion. A simple green salad makes an excellent accompaniment to this dish.

VARIATION
You could also sprinkle the balls with hard grated white cheese and serve them either as a sweet with icing sugar or as a savoury with salt and dotted with melted butter or lard. The potato balls can be filled, too: wrap little pieces of sausage or ground smoked meat in the mixture and fry in oil until they have a crispy shell. Serve them with fried rounds of onion, steamed spinach or a green salad.

Potato Pasta Balls with Powdered Poppy-seed (below), or with Fried Bacon and Onions

BAKED BARLEY (BLACK BARLEY)

- *20 g dried mushrooms*
- *300 g pearl barley*
- *salt*
- *100 g lard*
- *caraway*
- *a few cloves of garlic*
- *marjoram*

❶ Soak the mushrooms in cold water for an hour.
❷ Rinse the barley, cover with water in a pan, add salt and two tablespoons of melted lard and boil until soft. Boil off the water.
❸ Stew the mushrooms with salt and caraway until soft, and boil off the juice.
❹ Rub a baking dish with lard. Mix the barley with the mushrooms, the rest of the melted lard, the garlic mashed with salt and the marjoram. Spread the mixture in the baking dish and bake. Serve with sauerkraut salad (recipe on p. 22) or pickled cucumbers.

HASH

- *1 kg peeled potatoes*
- *salt*
- *100 g split barley*
- *80 g lard*
- *approx. 300 ml milk*
- *several cloves of garlic*
- *marjoram*
- *2 medium onions*

❶ Cut up the potatoes and cover them with water, salt and boil until soft.
❷ Rinse the barley, cover with water in a pan, add salt and a tablespoon of melted lard, and simmer slowly until soft, sometimes adding a little milk.
❸ Drain the potatoes, mash them, and beat them with the hot milk into a smooth mash. Mix with the soft barley. Season with garlic mashed with salt and with marjoram.
❹ Slice the onions in rounds and fry them in the remaining hot lard.
❺ Decorate the hash on the plate with the fried onion and dot with lard. Serve with a green salad.
Note: Hash can also be served with boiled smoked meat (recipe on p. 6), heated smoked cuts or sausages.

Baked Barley (above) and Hash served with grilled sausage

43

GRIDDLE-CAKES WITH BILBERRY SAUCE

- *300 g medium flour*
- *20 g fresh yeast*
- *1 tablespoon castor sugar*
- *2 egg yolks*
- *pinch of salt*
- *approx. 450 ml milk*
- *oil for frying*

- *hard white cheese for sprinkling*

For the bilberry sauce
- *400 g bilberries*
- *approx. 200 ml milk*
- *castor sugar*
- *1 teaspoon cornflour*

❶ Sieve the flour. Crumble the yeast into a bowl, mix with sugar and a little warm milk. Cover the bowl and when the yeast rises, gradually add the egg yolks. Add salt and then flour and milk alternately, while working the mixture into a thick paste. Cover and leave to rise.

❷ Work the risen dough again, and then place large spoonfuls on a hot griddle rubbed with oil. Cook each pancake to a golden brown on both sides. Stack the cooked pancakes in a bowl on top of a pan with hot water.

❸ **The bilberry sauce:** Trim and rinse the bilberries, cover with water and stew. Progressively add milk (reserving a little on one side), and sugar to taste and stew a little longer. Dissolve the cornflour in the reserved milk. Then add the mixture to the bilberries and stir continuously until the sauce thickens.

❹ Spread the bilberry sauce on the pancakes and sprinkle with grated hard white cheese.
Note: Bilbery sauce is also good with unfilled yeast or cream-cheese dumplings (see recipe on p. 46), ordinary pancakes, omelettes and cakes. Or else you can mix together chilled bilberry sauce with sour cream or plain yoghurt, decorate it with fresh bilberries and serve it as a dessert, or tea time snack.

VARIATION
The raised pancakes can also be decorated with damson-cheese and soft cream cheese mixed with plain yoghurt or sour cream, or with soft cream cheese combined with the bilberry sauce. Or try mixing 50 g of rinsed oats or 150 g of coarsely grated apple and 1/2 teaspoonful of cinnamon into the pancake mixture. The finished pancakes can also be rolled in cinnamon sugar.

FRUIT DUMPLINGS
USING YEASTY DOUGH

- *400 g medium fine flour*
- *25 g fresh yeast*
- *1 teaspoon castor sugar*
- *approx. 200 ml milk*
- *pinch of salt*
- *flour for rolling out*
- *fruit (strawberries, apricots, bilberries, plums)*
- *hard white cheese*
- *icing sugar*
- *butter*

❶ Sieve the flour into a bowl. Crumble in the yeast, add the sugar, 2 tablespoons of warm water and a little flour, and mix into a paste. Cover the bowl and when the yeast has fermented, add salt and work into a dough with remaining milk. Dust with flour, cover and leave to rise.
❷ Turn out the dough on a board and cut it into pieces of the same size. Put fruit in the middle of each and wrap up in the dough. Leave the dumplings to rise for another 5 minutes, and then drop them into boiling water in batches and boil for 8–10 minutes depending on size.

❸ Lift the dumplings out of the water with a perforated wooden spoon and immediately puncture them a few times with a fork, to prevent them congealing.
❹ Arrange the dumplings on a serving plate, sprinkle with grated hard white cheese and sugar, and dot with melted butter.
Note: Use frozen fruit, damson-cheese or jam as an alternative filling. You could also sprinkle them with grated nuts, gingerbread, or bread-crumbs heated in butter. Plum dumplings taste good sprinkled with powdered poppy-seed. Serve unfilled dumlings with a fruit sause (e. g. recipe on p. 44).

VARIATION
Cream Cheese Dough: Gradually mix 50 g cream cheese into 2 egg yolks, add salt, 2 tablespoons of cornflour already dissolved in 50 ml of milk, and 100 g of semolina. Work the mixture into a thick dough, adding coarse flour if need be. Leave the dough in a cool place for half an hour. **Potato Dough:** Finely grate 400 g boiled potatoes, add salt, sprinkle on 2 tablespoons of cornflour and 50 g semolina, break an egg in the middle and work into a smooth dough. Add approx. 100 g coarse flour as necessary.

APPLE STRUDEL

- *150 g fine flour*
- *60 ml hot water*
- *pinch of salt*
- *1 teaspoon wine vinegar or lemon juice*
- *60 g fat*
- *flour for rolling*
- *50 g raisins*
- *4–5 medium large apples*
- *30 g grated nuts or grated gingerbread*
- *cinnamon sugar*
- *icing sugar*

❶ Sift the flour onto a board. In the water combine salt, the vinegar or lemon juice, and 2 tablespoons of heated fat. Pour it into a hollow in the flour and work into a thick dough using a knife with a blunt end. Cover with a warmed bowl.

❷ Peel and core the apples, and cut into thin slices. Rinse and drain the raisins.

❸ Roll out the dough into a thin sheet, and then carefully stretch it by hand until it is almost transparent. Place it on a tea-towel dusted with flour, trim the thicker edges and sprinkle with fat, nuts or gingerbread. Then place the apples on top, sprinkle with cinnamon sugar and raisins, and roll up using the tea-towel while brushing with fat.

Transfer the roll to a greased baking sheet, pinch the ends of the dough together to seal and place in an oven preheated to 210 °C and bake for 25–30 minutes.

❹ Cut the roll into diagonal slices while it is still warm and dust with sugar.

Note: The warmer the dough is, the more elastic it becomes. You can put it in a microtene bag and warm it over steam. On festive occasions the apple strudel is served decorated with cream.

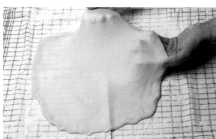

Roll out the dough into a thin sheet, and then carefully stretch it by hand.

Roll up the pastry filled with the apples and raisins using the tea-towel.

BAKED YEAST DUMPLINGS (BUCHTY)

- 400 g fine or medium flour
- 30 g fresh yeast
- 40 g castor sugar
- approx. 250 ml milk
- pinch of salt
- 60 g melted and then chilled butter
- 2 yolks of egg
- flour for rolling
- butter for greasing the baking tin and the dumplings
- damson-cheese

For the poppy-seed and damson-cheese filling
- 100 g powdered poppy-seed
- 50 ml hot milk
- 50 g damson-cheese
- 1 teaspoon cinnamon
- 1 teaspoon rum
- 1 teaspoon castor sugar
- cream cheese filling (see recipe on p. 52)
- poppy-seed filling (see recipe on p. 52)

❶ Sift the flour into a bowl, crumble the yeast into the middle, add the sugar, 2 tablespoons of warm milk and a little flour. Mix into a paste, cover and leave to rise.

❷ Add salt to the flour. Gradually add the butter, egg yolks and the remaining milk to the risen mixture, working it into a dough. Dust with flour, cover and leave to rise.

❸ **The poppy-seed and damson-cheese filling:** Scald the poppy-seed with the milk, mix with the damson-cheese, cinnamon, rum and sugar, and if necessary thicken with a little grated gingerbread.

❹ Place the risen dough on a board, work it smooth and cut it into pieces of the same size. Roll them into flat circles, add dollops of the filling and wrap them up in the pastry. Arrange dumplings in a buttered baking dish (don't crowd them), and spread a little butter on each.

❺ Let the dumplings rise for a further 10 minutes, and then put them in an oven preheated to 200 °C. After five minutes turn the temperature down to 180 °C and bake until golden.

❻ Take the dumplings out of the oven, separate them and leave to cool on a wire tray. When cool, dust them with sugar.

Note: These dumplings can be baked in various sizes. The smaller ones are served with coffee or tea. The larger ones used to be baked, filled with seasonal fruit and served for lunch after the soup.

VARIATION
Small unfilled yeast dumplings are also a favourite. They are baked in the oven in two layers to ensure that their edges are as little crisped as possible. Then they are served with runny vanilla custard flavoured with a little rum.

BOHEMIAN, CHODSKO AND MORAVIAN TARTS

- dough as for baked yeast dumplings (see recipe on p. 50)
- butter to grease tin
- raisins
- peeled almonds
- egg white for spreading

For the poppy-seed filling

- 100 g ground poppy-seed
- 100 ml hot milk
- 2 tablespoons melted butter
- 2 tablespoons castor sugar
- 1 tablespoon cinnamon

- pinch of ground cloves and star anise
- 1 teaspoon rum

For the cream cheese filling

- 40 g butter, melted and then chilled
- 1 sachet vanilla sugar
- 2 tablespoons castor sugar
- 1 yolk of egg
- 250 g soft cream cheese
- 2–3 spoonfuls milk

For the sugar crumbs

- 100 g medium flour
- 80 g castor sugar
- 60 g butter

❶ **Poppy-seed filling:**
Scald the poppy-seed with the milk and mix with the butter, sugar, spices and rum.

❷ **Cream cheese filling:**
Work the butter and vanilla sugar together with the egg yolk, gradually add the cream-cheese and milk and mix into a smooth paste.

❸ **Sugar crumbs:**
Sift the flour into a bowl, add the sugar and butter and work into fine crumbs with a blunt ended knife. Leave to harden in a cool place.

❹ **Bohemian Tart:**
Place the risen yeast dough on a board and knead it. Cut it into pieces of equal size, roll out into rounds and arrange on a buttered baking tin. Press a hollow into each using a jamjar, and fill the hollows with various fillings. Put three raisins on each cream-cheese tart, and a split almond on each poppy-seed or damson-cheese tart.

❺ **Chodsko Tart:**
Cut the dough in half and roll out into circles. Place them on buttered baking sheets. Put the fillings on the dough base in alternating rounds. Decorate with raisins and almonds.

❻ **Moravian Tart:**
Cut the dough into small pieces of equal size, roll them out in squares, add a dollop of filling and wrap in the dough like a yeast dumpling. Carefully press down the filled dough with a glass or weight, and add a different filling on top. Sprinkle the tarts with sugar crumbs and arrange on a buttered baking sheet.

❼ Brush the edges of the dough for the Bohemian and Chodsko tarts with beaten white of egg. Place the baking sheets in an oven preheated to 200 °C and bake until golden.

FRUIT PASTRIES MADE WITH YEASTY DOUGH

- *dough as for baked yeast dumplings (see recipe on p. 50)*
- *butter to grease tin*
- *sugar crumbs (see p. 52)*
- *fruit (bilberries, apricots, plums, redcurrants, cherries, gooseberries)*
- *ground poppy-seed*
- *castor sugar*

Note: The fruit can be arranged on the dough in different coloured lines. In winter you can use frozen fruit (but leave the dough to rise with the fruit for a little longer before putting in the oven), or well-drained stewed fruit. The tart can be made in circular tins as well, and cut into segments when cool. Sugar crumbs can be flavoured with cinnamon or desiccated coconut. Leftover tart can be frozen; take it out of the freezer an hour before you need it and let it thaw at room temperature.

❶ Place the risen yeast dough on a board, knead, roll out in a circle and transfer to a buttered baking tin, pressing out the edges to the sides.

❷ Scatter bilberries or redcurrants, cherries or gooseberries on the dough and add sugar crumbs.

❸ Stone the apricots, halve and lay on the dough in closely packed rows, cut side up. Sprinkle with sugar crumbs.

❹ Stone the plums, slice and arrange on the dough as for apricots. Sprinkle with sugar crumbs or with poppy-seed and sugar.

❺ Leave the dough with the fruit to rise for another 5 minutes. Then put the baking tin in an oven preheated to 200 °C and bake until the edges of the dough are golden.

❻ Turn the tart out of the tin while still hot, and cut into squares or rectangles when cool.

Transfer the dough to a baking tin and press it out to the edges.

Place the sliced fruit in close-packed lines on the dough.

THE EASTER LAMB

- *300 g medium fine flour*
- *½ sachet of baking powder*
- *4 yolks of egg*
- *100 g castor sugar*
- *1 sachet of vanilla sugar*
- *100 ml oil*
- *approx. 100 ml milk*
- *4 egg whites*
- *50 g castor sugar*
- *oil and flour for the form*

For the frosting
- *2 egg whites*
- *approx. 250 g icing sugar*

Note: The lamb can be made from yeast dough as well (see recipe on p. 50). You can replace the white frosting by a dusting of sugar. Or try chocolate icing, made by dissolving 100g of bitter chocolate with 30g of hardening fat in a bain-mari, and while the icing is setting, sprinkle with grated coconut. Whatever icing you use, give the lamb a red ribbon as finishing touch.

❶ Sift the flour with the baking powder.

❷ Cream the egg yolks with the castor and vanilla sugar, dribble the oil into the mixture and beat until light. Gradually add the flour and milk.

❸ Whip the whites of egg and castor sugar until stiff, and mix lightly into the yolk mixture.

❹ Pour the mixture into a buttered cake form, dusted with flour. Place in an oven preheated to 190 °C and bake. When half-cooled, ease the cake out of the form and place on a cooling tray.

❺ **Frosting:** Whip the egg whites, gradually add the sieved icing sugar and stir until the frosting is glossy and thick. If it is still too runny, add more icing sugar.

❻ Coat the cooled lamb with the icing. When the first coat is dry, put the remaining frosting into an icing bag (or just a plastic bag with a small hole), and decorate the lamb.

ADVICE

On Good Friday Czechs bake traditional Easter buns – made from yeasty dough (see recipe on p. 50). Roll the pieces of dough into tubes and then into pretzel shapes (see the photograph). Arrange the buns on a baking sheet and leave them to rise for 5 minutes. Then brush them with beaten egg and bake them until golden in an oven preheated to 200 °C. When the buns have cooled, dribble honey on them and serve them with coffee or tea as a Lenten lunch.

Easter Lamb and Easter Buns

CHRISTMAS CAKE WITH RAISINS AND ALMONDS (VÁNOČKA)

Number of Portions: 8–10   ✳ ✳ ✳

- 600 g fine or medium flour
- 42 g fresh yeast
- 100 g castor sugar
- approx. 200 ml milk
- salt
- 2 yolks of egg
- 1 sachet of vanilla sugar
- a little grated nutmeg
- 125 g melted butter
- 100 g raisins
- flour for rolling
- butter for greasing baking sheet
- 1 small egg for brushing
- almond flakes for decoration

❶ Sift the flour into a bowl. Crumble the yeast into a mug, add 2 tablespoons of sugar and flour, mix with a little warm milk and cover.

❷ Add a pinch of salt to the flour. Add the fermented yeast, egg yolks, remaining sugar, vanilla sugar, and nutmeg. Work into a thick dough while alternately adding milk and butter. Dust with flour, cover, and leave to rise. Knead the dough twice during the rising process.

❸ Rinse the raisins and drain thoroughly.

❹ Put the risen dough on a board, knead in the raisins and divide into nine equal parts. Roll them into thin rolls. Plait four rolls to make a braid, transfer to a buttered baking sheet and press the braid down firmly along the top. Make another braid out of three more rolls, place it on top of the first braid and once again press it down firmly. Twist together the last two rolls, place on top of the others and fold the ends down under the braids.

❺ Leave the dough to rise for a further 15 minutes. Then brush with beaten egg, sprinkle with almond flakes and place in an oven preheated to 220 °C. After 8 minutes lower the temperature to 190 °C and bake the Christmas cake until golden. Test whether it is ready by inserting a skewer (which should come out dry). Transfer the cake to a wire tray and let it cool.

VARIATION

You can use the same dough to make an Advent Garland. Cut the risen dough into three parts, roll them into long thin cylinders and plait them into a braid. Transfer the garland to a greased flan tin. When it is ready, dust it with sugar and decorate with a ribbon and Advent candles.

*The base of the cake is made from four rolls,
three rolls on the middle and two on the top.*

*Brush the cake with beaten egg, and
sprinkle with almond flakes.*

CHRISTMAS GINGERBREADS (PASTRIES)

✳ ✳

- 300 g fine flour
- ½ sachet of baking powder for pastries
- 50 g honey
- 100 g castor sugar
- 80 g butter
- 1 egg
- 1 teaspoon cinnamon
- ½ teaspoon ground cloves and star anise
- flour for rolling
- butter for greasing sheet
- frosting (see recipe on p. 56)

❶ Sift the flour with the baking powder. Heat the honey, sugar and butter together in a bowl over hot water, and then add to the flour. Add the egg and spices, and work to a dough. Cover and leave in a cool place for at least an hour or overnight.

❷ Roll out the dough and cut out shapes using Christmas forms. Arrange the pastries on a buttered baking sheet and bake in an oven preheated to 190 °C. Immediately turn them out to cool and when cold decorate with frosting (see p. 56).

Note: Use an icing bag to decorate the pastries with frosting. Icing can be difficult, since the frosting needs to be just the right consistency, neither too thick or too thin. Simpler effects can be achieved applying the frosting with a toothpick.

VARIATION
You can brush the pastries with beaten egg before baking and decorate them with halved walnuts, hazelnuts, almonds or candied fruit. If you want to use them as Christmas Tree decorations, make a hole in them with a skewer before baking.

Cut out the pastries from the rolled out dough using Christmas forms.

Decorate the pastries with white frosting using simple motifs.

THE FESTIVE YEAR

SHROVETIDE

The period from Epiphany to Ash Wednesday was always the merriest part of the year in the Czech Lands. It was a time of pig-slaughtering at home, because the frosty weather made it possible for a great quantity of meat and lard to be processed. The first and most popular delicacy at a pig-feast was boiled meat from the pig's head, served with horseradish. Soup made from pig's blood and barley was also served, and sometimes goulash including the pigs kidneys and liver. Sausages made of liver, blood and meat would all follow, eaten with home-made sauerkraut. The leftovers of meat would be salted and smoked, mostly in home-made salami. At Shrovetide people feasted and made merry – frying doughnuts, drinking beer, home-distilled liquor and wine, and holding masked balls. It culminated in the carnival procession on Shrove Tuesday. Ash Wednesday ended the period of merriment and life became calmer. The change was obvious in diet, since Lenten fare often included meatless dishes made of pulses with dried fruit and pickled cabbage.
The Spring festivals approached.

EASTER

The first Easter celebrations were still in Lent. Buns of yeasty dough, dipped in honey, were served for lunch on Good Friday. Often they were religious in symbolism – twisted like a rope recalling the crucifixion of Jesus Christ – or in the form of little birds symbolising the coming Spring. Only with Easter Sunday did people truly feast, for example on roast lamb, veal and a pudding made of eggs, smoked meat and plenty of green leaves and herbs. People used young nettle leaves, stewed like spinach, and made salad from young dandelion leaves. Even the poorest table boasted a lamb of yeasty or ordinary dough, and sticky Easter pastry with raisins and almonds.

WEDDINGS

were another opportunity for revels. Special wedding food included little tarts, not more than mouthfuls, made of yeasty dough and butter, mixed with cream to keep soft. They had all kinds of fillings, and were decorated with raisins, nuts and almonds. The bride would give them to all her neighbours, and they were part of the wedding hamper.

CHRISTENINGS

were joyful occasions in the family. Female neighbours would visit the new mother and bring her strong chicken soups with home-made noodles, and also tarts, buns and rolls made of yeasty dough in the form of a baby, with poppy-seed or nut stuffing and sprinkled with sugar crumbs.

HARVEST FESTIVAL

was a welcome celebration after hard work, and a thanksgiving for a good harvest. The farmers were satisfied to see the corn in the barns and their wives would make tarts with fillings, dumplings and dough-nuts. Roast fowl was on the table. In poorer districts pancakes stuffed with stewed cabbage or damson-cheese would be served instead.

WAKES

are still held in some villages and towns, although today they involve no more than a meal. They were held on the feast of the saint to whom the local church was dedicated. Guests at lavishly spread open-air tables would enjoy roast poultry and rabbit, or meat with cream sauce. Tarts and other sweets would be baked according to local customs.

FAIRS

were usually held at the end of a phase of agricultural labour in the fields and garden, at harvest-times. The noisy merry-making often lasted several days. The high point of the feast would be a fair goose with dumplings and cabbage. It would be preceded by the essential soup – a stock made of giblets and home-made garnish. When leaving the guests would be given a hamper, mainly of tarts and leftovers of roast poultry.

CHRISTMAS

is celebrated to remember the birth of the Saviour, but also the winter solstice. In The Czech Lands Christmas Eve is above all a family occasion. Traditionally, a fast all day was followed by an evening meal starting with black groats (barley), a delicacy made of dried mushrooms and groats lavishly larded and seasoned with garlic. This was followed by pea soup, and various purees flavoured with honey. In areas rich in fish,

carp would be served, although in a much humbler form than it takes on the Christmas table today. Then people would eat fresh fruit, mainly apples, traditionally associated with various customs and superstitions. Dried fruit and nuts were always accompaniments to Christmas as symbols of abundance. Richer food would be served at later feasts in the Christmas period – roast poultry, Christmas cake, small Christmas pastries and biscuits.

NEW YEAR'S EVE AND NEW YEAR'S DAY

At midnight on New Year's Eve, people would serve a slice of pork meat, and an ear and a snout if left over from a pig-killing. People believed that a piece of little pig brought good fortune. And also that eating lentils would ensure enough money. One cycle had ended and another began.

INDEX

How demanding the recipe is:

✳ Easy   ✳ ✳ Slightly complicated   ✳ ✳ ✳ Complicated

Copyright © Slovart Publishing, Prague 2000, 2004, 2009, 2013, 4th arranged edition
Text © Lea Filipová, Prague 2000, Photography © Jiří and Blanka Poláček, Zdeněk Lhoták
English Translation © Anna Bryson, Editor Jana Steinerová and Jana Klepetářová
Production Dana Klimová, Typography and lithography Atelier Degas, Druck Graspo CZ, a. s., Zlín
ISBN 978-80-7391-788-3

www.slovart.com